A Great Attitude

Today is going to be a great day!

Oh, no! My shoelace broke.

Oh, well. I will fix it.
I will have a great attitude.

Today is going to be a great day!

Oh, no! My milk spilled.

Oh, well. I will clean it up.
I will still have a great attitude.

Today is going to be a great day!

Oh, no! My folder ripped.

Oh, well. I will tape it.
I will still have a great attitude.

Today is going to be a great day!

Oh, no! My seat is taken.

Oh, well. I will find another one.
I will still have a great attitude.

Today is going to be a great day!

Oh, no! My desk is messy.

Oh, well. I will make it neat.
I will still have a great attitude.

Today is going to be a great day!

Oh, no! My friend is sick at home.

Oh, well. I will make a new friend.
I will still have a great attitude.

Today I had many problems.

Sometimes it's hard to have a great attitude.

But today was still a great day.
Do you know why?

Because I made it a great day!